KING OF THE RANGES

This edition published 2017
By Living Book Press
147 Durren Rd, Jilliby, 2259
Copyright © The Estate of C.K. Thompson, 1950

The publisher would like to give a huge 'Thank You' to the author's family
for their assistance in making this book available once more.

National Library of Australia Cataloguing-in-Publication entry:
Creator: Thompson, C.K. (Charles Kenneth), 1904-1980
Title: King of the ranges : the saga of a grey kangaroo / C.K.
                  Thompson.
ISBN: 9780648035688 (paperback)
Target Audience: For primage school age.
Subjects: Kangaroos--Australia--Juvenile fiction.
                  Nature stories, Australian.
                  Adventure stories, Australian.
                  Australia--Juvenile fiction.

KING OF THE RANGES

THE SAGA OF A GREY KANGAROO

By C.K. Thompson

20 17 LIVING BOOK PRESS

Contents

CHAPTER I.

EARLY DAYS

IT was somewhere in the woody country on the western side of the Great Dividing Range that Joey first saw the light of day, but his earliest recollections were of a little reed-edged creek many miles to the east of his birth-place, on the opposite side of the range.

He was almost twelve months old before his mother would allow him to remain out of her pouch for long. One balmy spring day, when the air was filled with the songs of birds and the chirping of insects, and flooded with warm sunshine which penetrated his fur coat and made him feel that he could hop along by the side of his old grey mother all day, she allowed him his longest freedom. As yet his legs were not strong enough to support his growing body for any length of time, but he was getting stronger each day.

The old kangaroo had not stirred far from the banks of the creek or the surrounding bush since she had arrived there with Joey months before. The grass was long and green, and the stream itself would be trickling merrily over its pebbles for sometime to come. In the middle of summer it would dry up, and its bed would become cracked and hard, but the winter rains had converted it now into a bubbling, running, little torrent.

Yes, time enough to move on when the hot summer withered the green grass and turned the creek into a chain of dry holes.

Under his mother's ever-watchful eye, Joey skipped along the creek bank, pausing now and then to nibble a tasty shoot. When he attempted to stray beyond her sight, the old grey mother hopped after him and gently turned him back.

As the balmy spring days fled, Joey and his mother slowly moved along the stream, lazing away the time during the day, feeding at sundown, and when night came on, retiring to some secluded woody glen where Joey, warmly snuggling deep down in the maternal pouch, would listen to the breeze stirring the branches of the high gums, and prick up his ears at the mournful cry of the wandering mopoke or the angry chattering of some vagrant opossum, before he finally buried his little black nose into his mother's warm fur and drifted off to sleep.

It was early in the summer when they finally left the little stream. The sun was getting hotter every day, and already the stream was beginning to dry up. Joey did not want to leave the creek at all. It was the only world he knew, and it was good enough for him. It was a rebellious little kangaroo that snuggled into his mother's pouch as she progressed through the scrub in the direction of the distant belt of woods which divided the range from the plains.

They did not make much progress during the days that followed. Joey was growing fast, and was becoming a burden to his mother. It was not long before she forced him to use his own legs quite a lot and, after the first few days, Joey did not mind in the least.

At the end of a week they were many miles from Joey's little creek, making for the open plains, near which his mother had spent most of her time before Joey came. She had left the plains in the winter for the little creek, knowing by instinct that nature would make ample provision there for her while Joey was a baby.

It was not only the knowledge that Joey was coming that had driven the old kangaroo from the plains at that particular time. Nor was it on account of lack of food and water, of which there had been sufficient. These things happened in the normal course of events. She was thankful that the real cause —the advent of a party of white human beings, with their terrible guns, dogs and horses, bent on depriving every kangaroo of its winter fur—did not happen in nature's ordinary round. It had been the second occasion on which she had had experience of white men, and she had no wish to repeat it.

Joey's mother did not know that kangaroo drives were very popular just then among the white men with their dogs and horses. Had she known, she might have felt apprehensive of returning to the plains so soon, especially as she now had Joey; or she may have merely twitched her ears disdainfully, and placed full reliance in her native instincts to care for herself and her little one.

Three weeks after leaving the creek, Joey saw his first human being. By this time he and his mother were approaching the mountains that divided the plains beyond from the bush on their side, and the old mother kangaroo knew that it was here that blacks might be encountered. She was extremely cautious during the daytime, never allowing Joey to stray at all from her side for fear that he should encounter some prowling blackfellow, whose cruel spear or swift boomerang would quickly end her little one's life.

Joey could not understand the restraint. Before this, he had been allowed to hop about by himself to forage for tender leaves and young shoots, but now that his mother insisted on his remaining at her side, his joy in life was dampened considerably. He decided to put an end to this state of affairs as quickly as possible.

His chance came sooner than he had anticipated. They had reached a small waterhole in the midst of a clearing, and his mother, thirsty after her long journey under the hot sun, pricked up her ears eagerly. She did not hop to the water at once. Such a course might be fraught with danger, as she did not know who or what might be lurking in the bushes.

Cautiously she made her way round the pool, with Joey following. Satisfied that all was well, and giving Joey a warning glance to impress upon him that he must not stir from the shelter of the friendly little shrub under which he was crouching, she hopped silently to the edge of the water and eagerly dipped her lolling tongue into it.

Back in the bushes, Joey knew that his chance had come. A few swift little hops carried him back the way they had come, and then he turned and went through the trees at a tangent.

It was at the edge of another clearing that he got his big surprise. Sitting around a curious, gleaming, darting object were several queer, two-legged creatures, with long paws, in which they were holding long sticks of wood. Joey's little ears quivered with excitement, while he sat back on his tail with his little black nose in the air.

There were four blackfellows in the party, and they were arguing loudly on the merits of the boomerang when matched against the spear. They were oblivious of Joey, who instinctively slipped out of sight and hid in some bushes from where he had an uninterrupted view of the proceedings.

As he watched, he saw a fifth blackfellow come

through the bushes on the opposite side of the clearing and join his companions. He was followed by a curious four-legged animal which was sniffing the air suspiciously. Joey was excited. Human beings, fires, dogs! He did not know what they were, of course; but he did not regret having left his mother when he could have such adventures as this.

The dog, too, was excited, but the cause was different. A wild-looking, half-tamed dingo, it was running round the clearing with its nose to the ground. It had scented Joey.

And it was just when Joey had decided to return to his mother that the dog saw him, and gave tongue. The blackfellows stopped their argument and sprang to their feet as one. Following the dog, they dashed at Joey with loud shouts.

Thoroughly scared, the little kangaroo fled through the bushes and over the logs with the shouting and barking pack after him, a terrified look in his brown eyes and his little tongue lolling out in his fright. It was the fastest he had ever moved in his short life, and he was not used to it.

Hopping madly through the trees and scrub, he hurled himself into an open space and then, with a cry of almost human joy, flung himself to the side of his mother, who stood erect near a blackened stump on the opposite side.

Louder shouts came from the pursuers when they

saw the old kangaroo, which stood, a proud and fiercely defiant figure, reared up to her full height. The dog made an immediate rush at her, and the men hung back to see the fun. They had witnessed several encounters in the past between their curs and kangaroos at bay, and, even though their brutes were invariably worsted in the contests, they were always willing to witness another bout.

Joey shrank panting to the ground behind his mother, who stood rigidly awaiting the onslaught. One excited blackfellow levelled a spear, but it was rudely knocked aside by another, and then the five of them egged on the dog with encouraging cries.

The brute went to its task enthusiastically, but its enthusiasm was rudely shattered when a sharp blow from a flying front paw knocked it head over heels.

The old kangaroo sprang backwards, trampling on the terrified Joey as she did so. The dog, with foaming jaws and snapping fangs, gathered itself for another leap, and flew straight at her breast. Once again the flashing paws sent him flying backwards, and this taught him caution. He began to circle round the panting kangaroo, his wicked little blood-shot eyes watching for an opening. It came, and it was Joey who unwittingly provided it.

The little kangaroo tried to wedge himself between his mother's legs and was flicked aside by her big tail. As she did this, she turned her head ever so slightly as if in apology, and in that instant the cur sprang again, effectually to bury his fangs into the old mother's furry chest.

A spasm of pain shot through the gentle creature and roused her to great anger. Seizing the dog with her front paws, she held him tightly, and then, raising herself on her huge tail and using each leg, armed with that single razor-sharp claw, she ripped the maddened brute from throat to tail and hurled him from her. The brute fell gasping to the ground and writhed in his death agonies.

With her ears upraised and her body trembling, the old kangaroo stood panting and awaiting the next onslaught. The five blacks redoubled their yells, and then hurled their spears as one. Three found their marks in that furry chest, already blood-red from the dingo cur's assault, and from his own life's blood which had gushed on her as she dealt the fatal blow.

With a shuddering sigh, she slipped sideways and sank to the ground, while the blackfellows, with shouts of glee, gathered around her to complete their deadly work.

Joey, knocked sideways by his mother's tail, had fallen into a dense patch of bracken where he now lay hidden. Disregarding his whereabouts, and forgetful for the moment that it had been he who had led them to the old kangaroo, the blacks were engrossed in the task of making sure that she was quite dead.

Silently and fearfully, Joey slipped from the bracken and hopped swiftly away into the bush. He did not pause until he had put several miles between him and the scene of death. It was not until much later that the blacks remembered him, but, after discussing briefly the chances of running him down, they resolved to console themselves with his mother. Food was not scarce, and the average blackfellow does not kill just for the sake of it.

As yet, Joey did not understand the full meaning of what had occurred in the glade. In his dim animal way he sensed that all was not as it should be, and decided that, after waiting around a bit, he would return and join his mother.

Nightfall found him several miles from the spot, but he was sure of the way back. A faint glimmering among the trees met his gaze as he hopped along towards where he expected to find his mother. The blacks had made a fire on the spot and were regaling themselves with kangaroo steaks before moving off to pick up the rest of their tribe.

Before Joey reached the fringe of the bushes around the glade, he raised his head and sniffed the air. He could detect that scent with which he had become acquainted for the first time that day—the scent of man, and, although he could not see them, and did not know the meaning of the glare from the fire, he realised instinctively that where that scent was there was danger—danger from those awful two-legged black creatures and their four-legged animal.

Terrified now that he could not find his mother, and not daring to approach closer, the little kangaroo turned round and hopped off among the trees. He felt terribly lonely. An offensive opossum swore at him as he passed, and a mournful mopoke croaked dismally. These noises were familiar to him, but they merely emphasised his loneliness and fear. Hitherto he had been able to afford to treat these night creatures with disdain, safe in the knowledge that his mother was there to protect him. Now that he was alone, however, he did not know what might happen to him.

Once or twice, as he progressed, he caught the faint scent of man on the night breeze and, after hesitating each time he smelled it, always turned in the opposite direction. It was the first time in his life he had travelled at night; in fact, it was the first time he had ever been alone at night. He was afraid—and he was lost.

The rising moon at length made things a little easier for him and, after travelling a few more disconsolate miles, he entered a patch of bracken fern and dropped down, on the ground, tired, lonely and frightened. Far to the left of him a bittern boomed, while in a high gum over his head two opossums fought and held high revel. One of these commenced to chase the other, which ran down the tree trunk to the ground, swearing horribly. Joey sprang up and hopped away until he came to another fern patch, into which he sank exhausted.

The risen moon flooded the quiet bush with a soft light. No longer were the noisy opossums disturbing the neighbourhood, while the bittern had moved on. Joey's tired little ears drooped, and he sank into a fitful slumber.

CHAPTER II.

THE WHITE MEN

THE fern patch was not far distant from the banks of a small creek, and along this was good grass. Joey, the terrors of the night behind him, had his fill of food and drink before the sun had risen, and slowly made his way along the stream towards the distant hills.

In a vague way he sensed that his mother had intended crossing those hills, as they had been travelling towards them when they had encountered the black men. His mother, he remembered, a little too late, had been right always, so there must be something very attractive in those hills, or on the other side of them.

For two days he made his way along the creek, which, as he progressed towards its source, dwindled into a mere narrow brook. He did not meet any creature that was likely to harm him; in fact, apart from a few snakes, a goanna or two, and a solitary rabbit, all of which treated him with indifference, the bush seemed to be devoid of wild life.

He had not sniffed that unpleasant man-scent on the breeze for several days, and the memory of it was being relegated to the back of his small brain. Night now held no terrors for him, as he had learned that there was nothing among the bush creatures likely to harm him.

It was on the fifth day after his mother's death that he again encountered man. By this time he had reached the foothills. The stream which he had been following died away, and at length he emerged from the bush and began to strike into the hills.

With difficulty he made his way over the rocks and boulders, hopping laboriously from one to another, but heading upwards always. At one stage he was interested to see a creature like himself, and yet not like himself—rather, a small edition of his mother, for Joey did not know what he himself looked like. This animal, a rock wallaby, was hopping from stone to stone, and, when it sighted Joey, it hopped over a rise and vanished. Joey set off after it, but he could not negotiate the rocks and crags like the wallaby, and did not see it again.

It was while he was making his way up a gully that he smelt that hated man-scent. It came, wafted on a gentle breeze, from the direction of the head of the gully. Joey paused and looked ahead, but could see nothing. He made a few cautious hops forward and then suddenly heard a loud bang and felt a stinging pain in the right leg.

As he turned to flee, he heard a shout, and, looking up the gully, saw a man running towards him. He noted with surprise that the man was different to the men who had killed his mother. This man's skin was white in parts—his hands and his face —but the rest of his body puzzled Joey.

But he did not stay to examine closely this interesting phenomenon. Instead, he hopped away down the gully as fast as his legs could take him. Near the bottom, he hopped to the right over some rocks and did not stop until he could no longer smell the man-scent.

The bullet which had been fired at him had just creased his leg, and he licked the wound as he lay panting on the rocky ground. Here was a new terror for him to face.

He did not leave his hiding place among the rocks until the sun was sinking, and then a heavy thirst compelled him to move. The only water-hole he knew of, one which he had used earlier in the day, was in that very gully in which he had seen the terrible white creature.

The moon was shedding a pale glow on the bush when he came in sight of the waterhole, so long had he taken in his cautious way to reach it. Before entering the gully, he skirted a huge rock, and gazed down at the waterhole from behind it. What he saw reassured him. There were three rock wallabies and several other smaller animals drinking.

Joey was about to spring lightly on to a rock beneath him on his way down when he was startled by a loud noise—the same as he had heard earlier in the day when his leg had been injured. Instinctively he shrank back, but no pain came, and wonderingly he gazed down into the gully again. Two of the rock wallabies had gone, but the third lay at the side of the waterhole, and towards this he saw a man quickly walking.

As he watched from the shelter of his rock, he saw the man pick up the dead wallaby and go to where several more men were emerging from among the rocks which flanked the sides of the gully. They examined the dead wallaby, and then turned and vanished the way they had come.

Joey silently withdrew and hopped disconsolately away. It would be too dangerous trying to get a drink that night, he considered. He made his way back to his rocky hiding place, and there he passed an uneasy and thirsty night.

Next morning early he struck away into the hills in a different direction to the waterhole. The hot summer sun beat down upon him relentlessly. His tongue began to loll out and progress became increasingly slow. Wearily he hopped along over the rocks until he came to another gully. In this there was a small waterhole, and, so great was his need, that the young kangaroo, throwing all caution to the winds, hopped to it as fast as he could.

Skirting a small rock, he hopped clean over a fallen log, and there, right in his path, was a dog!

The dog was as surprised as he was, but was more equal to the occasion. It sprang at Joey with a fierce bark. Joey paused uncertainly and, as the dog began to circle round him, the kangaroo faced round, too, his heavy tail flopping in a series of bumps as he did so. All the while his heart was beating like a miniature steam hammer.

The dog did not attempt to attack him. It was not a full grown animal, and Joey could see that it was very different from the mongrel that had fought with his mother. It was a cattle pup and belonged to a party of white men who were camping, prospecting and hunting in the hills. It had lost track of its master when it had wandered off on its own, and, reaching the gully, had lain down in the shade of the log for a rest before going in search of him.

Being a pup, it acted like one. Barking ferociously, it made at Joey, who trembled with fear. If the pup intended Joey to play with it, it was sadly disappointed. Joey did not want to play with a dog, or with anything else. He wanted a drink, and he wanted to be miles away from this gully.

Deciding that the young kangaroo was a poor sport, the pup's attitude changed, and it began to snap at Joey's legs. Joey stood, uncertain how to act in this crisis, and then the pup made a spring at his chest.

It was instinct alone that prompted Joey to make a vicious smack at the dog with his front paw. The result was electrifying and satisfying. The dog fell backwards with a yelp of pained surprise and, picking itself up, rushed yelping up the gully with its tail between its legs, leaving Joey panting with astonishment and relief.

He gazed after the retreating dog with twitching ears and then, hopping swiftly to the waterhole, drank his fill.

The pup in its mad rush up the gully met its master, who, attracted by the barking, was intent on investigating the reason. Looking beyond the howling pup, he saw Joey drinking thirstily. Quickly grabbing the pup and stifling its yelps, he dived behind a rock and then peeped curiously out again. The wind was blowing towards him, and the kangaroo was quite unsuspicious. Joey, indeed, was unconscious of everything except the life-giving water.

Crouching behind the rock, the man took careful stock of the situation. He was unarmed, but, even so, he shrank from shooting what was obviously a young kangaroo.

"I'd like to trap that young 'roo. It would make a great pet for the kids at home," he whispered to the pup, which was not interested. It had had enough of Joey and did not desire that the acquaintance should be continued.

Joey, having quenched his thirst, began to crop the grass at the edge of the pool. The man behind the rocks watched him thoughtfully and then surveyed the surroundings. He saw that he was in a natural cul-de-sac. If he could get round the kangaroo and run it up to the end where he now was, there was small chance of its being able to scale the almost perpendicular walls.

Keeping a tight hold on the restless pup, he

climbed the rocks at the back of him, and presently gained the top of the ridge. He made his way along it in Joey's direction, being careful to keep hidden along the rocks and scrub. The strong breeze still. blew in his direction.

Reaching his mate, Jack Brown quickly told him what he had in mind. Together they skirted the bushes and gained the bottom of the gully. Looking towards the waterhole, they noticed that Joey was preparing to move.

Dropping the pup, Brown whispered to his mate, Harry Stone, to hug the right wall while he took the left. Then, shouting to the pup to "sool him up," they rushed at Joey.

Taken completely off his guard, Joey swung round and hopped swiftly up the gully until he came to the end. Baffled, and not knowing which way to turn, he faced round to meet the oncoming men and dog.

As he ran, Stone quickly unwound a length of rope which had already been formed into a noose, and, as the pup made a dive at Joey, Stone threw the rope unerringly. It circled Joey's head, was jerked tight, and in a moment he was struggling on the ground.

Being a young and inexperienced animal, Joey could do nothing but lie, a terrified heap, while the two men quickly passed other ropes around him. Kicking the excited and vindictive pup out of the way, they soon had Joey helplessly swathed in bonds.

A dead tree branch was run through the ropes and, each taking an end, they set off down the gully. Not long afterwards they were at their camp proudly exhibiting their capture to the three other men who completed their party.

"How do you expect to get him home?" asked one of the men. "You can't keep him trussed up like that all the time, and we haven't got any cage for him."

"I'll work that out later," said Brown.

"Why not let the poor thing go?" exclaimed the man.

"Not on your life," retorted Brown. "He's mine and he's going home as a pet for the kids."

Joey was dumped unceremoniously under a tall gum tree and the ropes partially untied. Immediately he began to kick and struggle madly for freedom, and one of the men kicked him roughly in the ribs, an action which brought a roar of protest from the man who had advised Brown to let him go. But the kick had the desired effect. The thoroughly terrified young kangaroo, its soft brown eyes dilated and its small black nose quivering, lay still except for slight twitching of the muscles.

Working quickly, Brown and Stone ran two ropes round a tree, tying the end of one round Joey's leg and the end of the other round his neck. Then they stood back and watched.

Springing up, Joey darted off, but was brought to a full stop by the cruel retarding ropes. The force threw him to the ground. He made several more attempts before he awakened to the futility of it, and then just lay in a heap on the ground at the end of the ropes, his sides heaving and his eyes wide and staring.

After watching him for a time, the men retired to the fire, around which they grouped and discussed the affairs of the day, while one of their number prepared the midday meal.

Throughout the long afternoon Joey was left under the tree. The man who had befriended him, he was little more than a youth, was then left behind to look after the camp—and Joey—while the rest of the party resumed their hunting and prospecting.

The young man, noticing Joey's plight in the hot sun, placed a billy of water near him, but the scared kangaroo did not heed it. He did not attempt to rise from the ground. A small lizard ran swiftly over the leaves near him, and in a nearby bush, two wrens twittered as they searched for insects for lunch. A butcher bird chattered in a high tree, while a curlew's weird cry sounded from the hills above him.

It was the call of the wild, and it found an echo in poor Joey's breast. Once again he made a hopeless struggle for freedom, and once again the ropes prevented him.

Nightfall, which heralded the return of the rest of the party, still found him lying under the tree. He was hungry and thirsty, lonely and scared. The men favored him with cursory glances as they made for their tents, and the young man remonstrated with Brown and pleaded with him to allow Joey to go free. But he was told curtly to mind his own business.

When it was quite dark, Joey commenced to struggle anew, but his efforts, as before, were unavailing. The men did not trouble him, and when at long last they sought their tents and their bunks, Joey had reached the conclusion that he would remain tied to that tree forever.

Sleep for him was, naturally, out of the question. He just lay on the hard ground, wide-eyed, too tired now to struggle against the bonds that held him. Then a movement in one of the tents attracted him, and he saw the young man creeping silently towards him.

With a great effort, Joey balanced himself on his hind legs and tail, and wrenched at the rope with what little strength he had left. The young man crept around him to the tree to which he was tied and swiftly undid the ropes.

Lying on the ground again, Joey did not realise that he was free until the man picked up a stick and threw it at him. He braced himself for another tussle with the ropes and almost overbalanced as he met with no resistance. In a few moments he was flying through the trees and rocks with the ropes trailing behind him. The one round his neck nearly choked him as it caught in passing obstacles, but the other, having worked loose during the struggles under the tree, finally fell off and was left lying on a log over which he hopped in his frantic flight away from that hateful camp.

When he had been tied to the tree, the leg rope had been the shorter, and had always brought him to a full stop in his efforts to get away, consequently the noosed one round his neck had never been allowed to tighten very much. It had not worried him to any great extent then, but now, as he shot through the bush, it caught in almost every projecting obstacle.

It was impossible for Joey to go far. He had been lying in the hot sun without water for most of the day, and much of his strength had been used up in his attempts to get free from the tree. He kept on for a few miles and then, coming to a cleft in a huge rock, sank to the ground inside, beaten, the rope still round his furry neck.

Lying on the ground, he worked his head in all directions like a fowl with its head caught in wire netting. He could not dislodge the rope, but he succeeded in loosening it until it hung around his throat like a necklace.

The late summer moon was sinking over the tree tops as he gave the problem up and sank into an exhausted slumber.

CHAPTER III.

THE MOUNTAINS

JOEY rid himself of the maddening rope in an unexpected manner. Early next morning he left the rock cleft and made his way up a rocky spur where he found a small pool of water in a shallow depression. The rope was hanging loosely round his neck, and the hole was deep. It was only by bending his body and stretching his neck to the fullest extent that he could reach the water, and, as he drank thirstily, the rope suddenly slipped off and fell into the water. Startled, Joey hopped away.

During the days and weeks that followed, he penetrated deeper into the mountains, without meeting with any adventures. His baby days on the banks of the little stream were almost forgotten now, and the death of his mother, two months before, was fading from his memory. Since that episode, his days had been so crammed with personal incident that he had had little time to spare to ponder over the past.

As he made his way deeper into the mountains, he wondered in a dim way whether there were any other creatures like himself. He met several rock wallabies as he progressed, but they avoided him. Joey was almost on the top of the mountains when he met trouble again.

It was late in the afternoon of the tenth day after meeting the white men that, while drinking at a small rock pool, he became aware of a number of animals approaching. Raising his head, he subjected them to a tense scrutiny. They were dogs. Not the kind of puppy that he had defeated just before the cruel white men had captured him, but yellow-looking beasts, faintly reminiscent of the cur that had attacked his mother.

There were five dingoes in the pack and, when they sighted Joey, they came to an abrupt halt. They could see that Joey was young, and they knew by instinct and from experience that where there was a young kangaroo, in nearly every instance there would be a mother also; and a mother kangaroo with a young joey was an animal to be dealt with circumspectly.

This being so, they did not launch an immediate attack as a pack of domesticated dogs would have done. Instead, they began to approach cautiously, and ever on the alert. Joey watched them for a moment, and then began to hop away, his head turned in their direction.

The dingoes came on slowly, following him among the trees, and, as they got further away from the waterhole, they realised that there were no adult kangaroos to be considered. They increased their pace and so did Joey. The dingoes began to string out. Two of them were elderly males, the third a female brute, all teeth, while the other two were well-grown young dogs; and it was from the latter pair that Joey had most to fear.

The going was very hard. Coming to a slope, Joey could not hop up it directly, so went at it at an angle. Behind him the silent dingo pack was gaining steadily, and before long the two leaders were snapping at his very heels. Presently he reached a narrow ledge with a sheer drop of several hundred feet below. He hopped cautiously along this ledge until suddenly he was brought to a halt by a towering wall. He was completely trapped.

With a savage bark, the first sound uttered since the pursuit began, the leading dingo sprang. Joey at the same time whirled round to face his enemies and, more by luck than design, managed to get in a sharp blow as the dingo was in mid-air. Backwards it went and, with a wild howl, vanished over the edge of the cliff, to strike the jagged rocks hundreds of feet below.

The second brute was a cowardly cur, and paused when he saw what had happened to his brother. Then, as the rest of the pack joined him, his spirits rose and he sprang at Joey's throat. Joey tried to meet the attack, and partly succeeded. Instinct prompted him to use his sharp hind claws, and he managed to slightly rip the dingo's side. The brute gave an agonised yelp and fell back a pace.

The rest of the pack then sat down on its several haunches and eyed Joey balefully, while the wounded leader licked its hurt, and sniffled. Joey, his back to the wall, awaited the next onslaught, but it did not come. Indeed, as Joey edged along the ledge a little in their direction, they all slunk back a pace or two.

It was then that help came to Joey from an unexpected quarter. On the other side of the cliff opposite the ledge a giant grey kangaroo appeared. It stood and looked across the chasm at Joey and his evil companions. The dingoes noticed it before Joey did, and there was a sudden scatter. The wild dogs did not pause to work out how the big kangaroo could cross the chasm to help Joey, but ran off into the bush.

Nothing was further from the mind of the newcomer. It had not the slightest intention of trying to cross. It stood on the edge of the cliff for a few seconds, gazing curiously at the departing dingoes, and then, throwing a side glance at Joey, wheeled round and vanished.

Joey, excited, hopped back along the ledge and, after a lot of seeking, managed to find a way down into the gully. It was harder work getting up the other side, but he managed it at last, and set off in pursuit of the big kangaroo. The thought of his mother came back to him with a rush, and, as she was the only other kangaroo he knew of, he felt certain that it must be her. But why she should run away instead of assisting him to beat off the wild dingoes was a question which puzzled his small brain.

He travelled until nightfall, but did not see the big kangaroo any more. That night he spent in a cave, and next morning he resumed his journey.

Joey spent several weeks in the mountains hunting for the other kangaroo, but he did not find it. Neither did he find any others of his kind. During this period he was a little hard put to it to get adequate food and water. Summer was on the wane and, as it had been a very severe one, grass and water in the mountains was far from bountiful.

It was in the early autumn that he reached the true summit of the mountain range, and gazed far out on the vast plains beneath him. As far as his eyes could reach was a great and seemingly bare expanse of country which appeared, from that distance, to be devoid of life, either animal or human.

Far away to the right he saw a shining ribbon of water, fringed with stunted trees, while to the left was a grassy expanse of open country.

This was the great plain to which his mother had been travelling!

Hastily Joey began to make his way down, thinking, no doubt, that he could reach the plains in a few hundred hops. In this he was sadly disappointed. Three days passed, and he was still making a laborious passage down the rocky, woody slopes, and the plains seemed as far away as ever.

Once he saw another kangaroo also, apparently,

making its way down from the mountains to the open country, but, when he attempted to join it, it quickly hopped away from him.

Then one day Joey saw a grand sight.

He had been following a deep gully which led gently downwards, and presently came across a trickling stream. After a long drink, he hopped along the bank until the stream dropped over a short precipice into another gully. The bottom of this gully was almost level, and led out on to the open plains.

It was getting dark when Joey reached this last gully and, as he rounded a rock, he saw a large pool of water, around which fully thirty kangaroos were drinking and grazing.

He had found his people!

Hesitantly he hopped forward, pausing now and then to take stock of them and to judge how he was likely to be received. They raised their heads, some of them, and viewed the newcomer, but made no demonstrations. Indeed, Joey, to them, was most unimportant, especially as he was not of their species. Joey hopped among them and began to search for his mother. In the failing light he approached an elderly kangaroo and nuzzled her flanks—to receive a sharp cuff over one ear for his impertinence. In confusion, he retired a few paces and wiggled the aching ear.

Suddenly a grand old kangaroo raised his head and stood perfectly still, except for a lightly-twitching ear. Then, without a sound, he wheeled away and commenced to hop swiftly towards the open plains. The other kangaroos followed him unquestioningly, leaving Joey standing there alone.

What was going on he had no idea, but he did get more than a glimmering of the truth when a rifle shot rang out and a bullet chipped the ground at his side.

How he remembered that hateful sound! In a very few minutes he was hopping swiftly after the retreating mob, and it was not long before he was keeping pace with the very leaders.

Total darkness found the mob far out on the plains where, the scare over, they began to scatter, feeding or sleeping as the mood took them. And where they went, Joey went, too, happy at last. He had found, if not his people exactly, at least his kind.

At first the other members of the band did not take too kindly to his presence. They were red kangaroos, the denizens of the plains, while Joey was a grey, a forest dweller. They did not molest him, nor did they display any active antagonism towards him; rather did they treat him with silent contempt.

Joey did not mind that. He needed companionship, so he stuck closely to the mob. There was food enough for all, and that, after all, was the main consideration.

And so, for the first time in his life, Joey had company of his own kind. He lived with the red kangaroos in the way that ducks and fowls congregate together in a suburban backyard.

CHAPTER IV.

THE KANGAROO DRIVE

AS the autumn advanced and the days grew shorter, the mob grazed slowly southwards, never out of sight of the ranges. With them went Joey, now an accepted member. There was still ample grass and water, and, with nothing to worry his small brain, Joey was as happy as any young kangaroo could be. There were plenty of youngsters of his own age in the mob, and Joey spent all his time in their pleasant company.

Whenever there was a hint of danger, or when night came down over the plains and his young companions sought the comfort of their mothers' sides, it was then that Joey felt lonely, but, as day succeeded day, he grew more and more self-reliant and self-sufficient. He had been thrown upon the mercy of a callous world long before nature had intended, but the need for a mother's protection had almost disappeared. Joey was now over two years old.

The first chilly blasts of winter, bringing with them the seasonal rains, found the mob of red kangaroos, and Joey, many miles southward, and the older members were more and more on the alert, especially at evening when they went to the waterholes. They were nearing the haunts of the white man, and many of the mob had lively recollections of the horrible drives when their numbers had been sadly reduced. During the last raid the settlers and others had not confined their slaughter to the reds of the plains, but had gone into the timbered lands and made war upon the greys —upon Joey's kin. Joey's mother had deserted her own mob very close to the spot where Joey had fallen in with his present red companions.

One day Joey's mob sighted a man on horseback. He was at a distance, and quickly sped out of sight. He was a scout, but the mob did not know that. As he quickly vanished over the far horizon, the kangaroos dismissed him from their calculations and immediately forgot him.

It was on the second day, early in the morning, that the tragedy occurred. The mob was scattered over half a mile radius, some quietly feeding, others just lazing on the ground, when over the southern horizon appeared a party of men on horseback, accompanied by a pack of howling dogs.

The leader of the kangaroos, a large old battle-scarred male, sighted the party while it was still a long way off.

He raised his wise old head and gazed like a graven image for several seconds, nose quivering, in the direction of the approaching men and dogs. With a queer little grunt he wheeled round, his large tail flopping on the ground several times, and was off like the wind. At this manifestation of danger, the younger kangaroos sought their mothers' sides, and, in a few seconds, the whole mob was in full flight.

Joey was the last to move off. He had not quite grasped the meaning of it all. He had encountered white men many months before, but his animal brain was not of abnormal strength. Though he knew enough, or remembered enough, to associate nasty things with men and dogs, he was at some loss to account for the hurried departure of his friends.

Instinctively he followed them, while the men drew nearer. Suddenly the breeze veered slightly, and Joey's sensitive nostrils caught that hated scent —man! He was in the middle of the mob within a few seconds, hopping for his very life, memories flooding his brain—men! dogs! ropes! bullets!

With those fleeing animals it was now each for himself, and heaven help the slow ones. Luckily there were no unfortunates—too large to occupy their mothers' pouches, and yet too leg-weak to keep up with the mob. Led by the old man, the kangaroos swept away, stringing out as they fled. The hunting party spread out also, gaining steadily on the slow ones. After about twenty minutes' breathless chase, the leaders of the dog pack were close enough to the stragglers, mostly the young members of the red mob, to make their first kill. Joey saw two large dogs spring upon a young kangaroo together, and bear him to the ground. And then some of the men opened fire with their guns. Three of the flying animals dropped in their tracks, but the rest kept on, panic lending wings to their fleet legs and bumping tails.

With one of the white horsemen almost on top of him, Joey swung away from the mob and set a course for the distant hills. As he drew away from his old companions, his ears were assailed by the sound of firing guns, yelping dogs, and the hoarse shouts of the human pursuers. He kept on going.

Close behind him rode the relentless white man. The dogs were busy to the rear with the now demoralised kangaroo mob, and Joey's pursuer had deserted his comrades to concentrate on the youngster.

How Joey hopped! Every second he expected to hear the terrifying sound of a discharged firearm, and to feel the stinging hurt of a bullet in his flesh, but it did not come. The man, riding behind, did not attempt to molest him. He meant to capture Joey, and had cut him out from the mob for just that purpose. Joey did not waste any time wondering why it was he had left the mob. All he realised was that once again he was alone, except for that hated hunter on his very tail.

The long chase began to tell on him, but he kept going. The ranges seemed as far away as ever, and eventually his pace grew slower and his hops shorter.

Suddenly the man spurted forward and in a few

moments was riding neck and neck with the flying kangaroo. For a few dizzy seconds Joey kept his pace up and then, when the man leaned forward in his saddle and dealt him a stunning blow on the head with the butt of his heavy stockwhip, Joey gave a shuddering sigh and went tumbling head over tail, ending in an unconscious heap in the dust of the plains.

He came to his senses in strange surroundings. His limbs were unfettered, yet he could barely move. He lay still for a moment, and then tried to heave himself to his feet. After a struggle, he managed it, but could hardly stand up straight, certainly not to his full height. He was in a cage. A bewildering array of wire netting enclosed him on every side.

All round him was hustle and bustle. Men went this way and that. Dogs barked, horses neighed and whips cracked. Joey trembled and winced involuntarily at the sound of those whips. They reminded him too much of rifle shots.

Through the meshes of the wire, Joey saw several of his erstwhile red companions in a similar plight to his own. On a long pole suspended between two tents he saw several more of his friends who would roam the plains no more. They were hanging, heads downwards, in grotesque attitudes, and, as he watched, he saw several men lift down a couple of the carcases and begin to skin them.

Joey was a prisoner in the camp of the hated white

men. The party had been searching for a kangaroo mob for some time with the object of capturing young ones alive. These unfortunates were destined for a life in a big public park. Joey did not know this, neither would he have understood nor cared if he had.

But another thing Joey did not know. He, himself, was not destined for a public park. He was the private property of the man who had caught him. The park party were after red kangaroos. Joey was a young grey, and the hunter had recognised him as such. He was already speculating on the joy Joey would cause in the heart of a small girl on a homestead further to the south. Joey's new master was a settler who had been engaged by the party of men to act as guide. His small daughter, learning the nature of her father's errand, had demanded imperiously that he bring her back a little kangaroo for her pet. Joey was hardly a baby, but that would not matter.

It was nearly a week later that Joey, after a wearisome journey, arrived at his future home. The settler, his cage slung on the side of his old packhorse, arrived at his home after dark. His small daughter was in bed, and he did not awaken her. Joey would provide a delightful surprise for her next morning.

Joey spent the night in the cage, which was placed in a shed. Next morning he was taken out into the sunlight and placed in a conspicuous spot in front of the homestead.

He had been there about half an hour when the

door opened, and a little girl, about five years old, suddenly burst forth. When she caught sight of Joey and his cage, she clapped her hands in great delight.

"Oh, you beautiful little kangaroo. Betty knew Dadda would bring you home to her," she cried, running eagerly to the cage.

Glaring at her balefully, Joey did not share her joy in this meeting.

Betty's father followed her from the house, smiling with pleasure at the little girl's obvious delight.

"Is your father any good now, Betty?" he said, with a grin.

"You are the best daddy in the whole world," cried the child, running to him and hugging his knees. He caught her up and swung her lightly to his shoulder, Joey watching the scene with dislike.

"You must not worry poor Joey now. He is frightened. Presently your old dad will make a nice yard for him, and, when he is quite tame, you may play with him and tie pretty ribbons round his neck," said her father.

How indignant that would have made Joey, had he understood what it was all about! Pretty ribbons round his neck, indeed!

"I want to play with Joey now," returned the girl, with a pout of her pretty little red lips.

"If I let him out he'll hop right away back to the mountains, and you won't have a pet Joey," said the settler patiently.

He put the child on the ground again.

"Now then," he said, patting her soft curls, "you run right inside again out of the cold and ask mummy to give you a nice breakfast."

Joey spent the next two days in his uncomfortable cage, but on the third he was given comparative freedom in a narrow yard enclosed by high wire netting. Immediately he was released he hopped madly away until he was brought to an unpleasant stop by the wire. The force of the impact threw him backwards. He made a circuit of the wire fully twenty times before he realised that he was effectively imprisoned, and then he retired into a corner and sulked for the rest of the day.

The wire netting had been run around a grass patch, in the corner of which was a small pool of water about a foot deep and two feet each way. The settler kept this filled for Joey, who did not appreciate any of these actions. Nor did he respond to the overtures of the settler and his wife during the days that followed. Joey had had quite enough of human beings and certainly had no intention of placing them on his list of friends.

He kept away from them when they entered his yard. The little girl was never allowed in the yard at all.

A miserable animal was Joey through these short winter days. Each night he made his monotonous round of the enclosure, ever hopeful, but he could not get free. And so the weeks passed. Eventually he gave it up as a bad job and resigned himself to his captivity. He even began to take a slight interest in the homestead itself. The settler's two dogs perturbed him for a long time, but he found out at last that, though he could not get out of his yard, neither could the dogs get at him. Not that they attempted to.

As time passed, he forgot his resentment of the settler when he entered the enclosure, and did not hop madly away as the man came near him. He resisted all efforts at fondling, however, and once, when the settler trapped him in a corner and patted him on the head, his resentment knew no bounds. The settler was knocked flying and Joey, still smarting under the indignity, hopped wildly round his yard three times, to the vast amusement of the family, including the settler himself.

Joey hated this man, but his hatred became passive. He gave up fighting off other advances and, as far as possible, kept himself within himself.

It was not until the settler tried partial starvation that Joey gave in. The grass in his enclosure had long since been eaten, and Joey had to depend upon grass and other food which was thrown to him. The settler left him without food for two days, and, on the third, when the man threw him an armful of thistles, Joey thought he had never tasted anything so delicious in his life. It was his first introduction to luscious thistles in bulk.

The next step in the taming process was another two foodless days, and then the settler entered the yard with a great handful of thistles. Joey saw him and prepared for insults. The man edged him into a corner and threw him a few thistles. Joey gazed at them askance for a few seconds, and then began to sample them, one eye kept as much as possible upon his master. He approved of the thistles and wished for more. The settler obligingly held them out to him. For a long, long moment Joey hesitated. The settler stood motionless. Joey stretched out his neck and then drew it back again. The man leaned forward and irritatingly tickled his nose with a bunch of thistles. He quivered slightly and then took a mouthful. In another few seconds he was actually eating out of a human hand.

After that it was easier. Joey was allowed some grass —not too much—but he could not have thistles unless he actually took them from the hands of either the settler or his wife. Sometimes he would refuse the offering altogether, and, when he did, it meant a foodless day for him. Gradually he began to realise what it all meant, and just as gradually he got into the habit of eating from the hand.

When the settler considered that Joey was tame enough, he introduced his small daughter with a bunch of thistles. Joey graciously accepted them.

The warm spring days came round and found Joey reconciled to a life of captivity. He was growing very fast, and his animal brain was starting to lose its conception of life in the wilds. The howl of a dingo which he heard one night stirred an unconscious echo somewhere deep down in his being and made him uneasy and a little restless, but it was the only call of the bush that he heard during his captivity.

Spring gave place to summer and summer to winter again, and Joey was still a prisoner. He was getting into his sixth year now, and growing bigger and bigger after the fashion of his species.

These days found him on good terms with his owners. No longer did he resent their advances. He even submitted to a piece of blue ribbon being tied round his neck by Betty, whose attentions he resented least of all. Be that as it may, he would not submit for long to this fondling. Deep down, there was a smouldering distrust of the whole human race. Dormant this distrust might be, but it was there.

Occasionally strange human beings would visit the homestead and attempt to make friends with him. These people he avoided as far as possible. He would not submit to their caresses and ignored their friendly gestures.

One of these visitors, a young fellow who always arrived on horseback accompanied by a dog, was Joey's pet abomination. This fellow persisted in cracking a whip, and that cracking whip reminded Joey of unpleasant things. The young man spent a great deal of his visiting time trying to make friends with the kangaroo, but Joey would have absolutely nothing to do with him.

One day Joey heard this young man arguing with the settler. He did not know, of course, that the argument concerned himself. His interest would have been aroused to fever-heat had he been capable of intelligently following the conversation, because the young man wanted to buy him from the settler.

"It can't be done, Jack," said the settler positively. "Joey belongs to Betty and she wouldn't part with him for all the rice in China. Why don't you go out on the plains and catch one yourself?"

The young man grunted.

"There is small chance these days of catching a young 'roo," he replied. "I've been north, south, east and west, and the plains are deserted because of the drives lately. I can't afford to go too far.

"Anyway," he went on, "that 'roo you have is a half-grown grey, and you won't find many of them about, not on this side of the range. There may be some in the bush on the other side, but I can't be bothered traipsing right over there. Look here, I'll give you a couple of pounds for him."

"Nothing doing, Jack. I'm sorry. Betty would never forgive me," said the settler, shaking his head.

"Funny, isn't it, that you found him among that mob of reds," said the young man thoughtfully.

"Driven out of the bush and hills by an old man, probably."

"I couldn't say," returned the settler. "It must have been something extra special, because greys always stick to the bush."

"They get around all over the place. But that's not the question. I didn't ride over here to discuss habits of kangaroos. Will you sell him to me? This is the last time I'll ask," said the visitor.

"No, I won't," retorted Joey's owner. "How many more times must I tell you?"

"Is that your final word?"

"Yes. Absolutely."

"All right, then. Keep him. I hope the thing dies on your hands," snorted the young man, springing on to his horse.

"Say, don't let us quarrel over the animal," begged the settler. "We've been friends too long for that."

"Will you sell him?"

"No!"

"Well, then, so long. I'll see you some more," grunted the visitor and rode away with his dog trotting after him and his whip cracking loudly—to Joey's disgust.

The settler came over to Joey's yard and looked at him affectionately. "Don't you worry, Joey, old boy. We won't sell you," he said.

Joey replied with a hoarse and uncomprehending cough, and went on browsing.

Late that night, as Joey was making a circuit of his enclosure in search of the young grass which grew near the bottom of the wire, he became aware of the prowling form of a human being making towards him, and knew it to be his whip-cracking enemy. Immediately, he sheered off to the opposite side of the yard, but the man did not heed him. A dog began to bark and, coming out from under the house, sniffed suspiciously at the intruder's legs. The man whistled softly and the growl died away, to be replaced by a wagging tail as the visitor, whom the dog now recognised, threw him a piece of meat. He had come prepared for this canine intervention.

Swiftly the young man gained the gate of Joey's yard and, with a deft movement, unlatched it and threw it wide open. In another moment he had vanished into the darkness.

Joey did not discover the opening until nearly dawn, and then only by accident.

He had given up all hope of freedom long ago, and, when he came to the open gate as he browsed around the bottom of the wire netting, he moved through the opening and into the yard without realising it. He hopped across the yard and fed on the grass beyond, and, when at length he paused and gazed idly around him, the homestead was a quarter of a mile away.

Understanding did not come to him at once. He looked around him once or twice, but continued to browse ahead until a sleepy dog, noticing him, began to bark in a tired fashion. The dog did not follow up the bark with pursuit, but the noise did make Joey hop a little faster.

By the time the sun was above the horizon, Joey was miles away, heading instinctively north—towards the bush, the ranges and the open plains.

CHAPTER V.

THE LONELY KANGAROO

THERE was consternation and excitement at the homestead when Joey was missed. The little girl was tearful, while her father made a hurried search of the vicinity of the property and especially the outlying cultivation. After a fruitless search of the corn and lucerne patches where he had hoped to find the missing kangaroo, he returned to the house, comforted his little daughter as well as he could and then, saddling his horse and whistling to his dogs to follow him, rode off in the direction of the ranges.

Joey, however, had had two hours' start, and, as he hopped onwards, old memories flooded his brain. There was a hint of spring in the crisp morning air, and, in spite of his long captivity, he felt very much alive, skipping and hopping, and sometimes frisking about to pick a tender shoot of grass, he was as free from care as only an animal can be.

It was the need for water that caused him to deviate towards a small clump of bushes that appeared to his right, and, sure enough, he found a pool. As he neared it, a blue crane rose and flapped away, while a pair of ibis, after regarding him fixedly for a few seconds, continued their wading in the shallow water as if he were beneath their further notice. The grass there was good, so Joey, after slaking his thirst, stayed in the vicinity for a time. He was in no hurry.

It was this deviation of the young kangaroo that undoubtedly saved him from recapture for, as the hunting settler rode along, his eyes eagerly scanning the horizon, he passed the clump of bushes away to his left. Joey was hidden in those bushes, but the settler did not even consider searching them. He was looking far ahead for a moving object, not thinking for one moment that Joey would linger around now that he had regained his freedom.

The sun was high in the heavens before Joey decided to leave the hospitable waterhole, and he travelled until sundown with hardly a pause. He did not hurry, but he kept up a consistent pace. He spent the night near a small waterhole in the shadow of the hills, and continued his journey as dawn broke.

Joey's adventures on his way home were few. Once he was scared by the appearance of two emus which followed him for about half a mile, but did not attempt to interfere with him. They were unfamiliar creatures to the kangaroo, so he did not stop to make their acquaintance.

After a week's steady going, Joey was in the foothills, but miles to the south of the spot where he had joined the red kangaroos. Something inside him, instinct probably, caused him to recall that mob to mind, and he decided to look for it. He did not know that, out of that original band of thirty, only seven now were left, and they were scattered over the plains. Further west, and far to the north, there were large mobs, but Joey did not know that. There were many things that Joey did not know.

Leaving the foot of the mountains, he struck off directly across the plains, though he could not have told why he did so. Nightfall found him at a waterhole ten miles out. There were half a dozen emus at the hole, and he quietly waited for an hour or more until they had gone before he ventured to drink. He did not know what these creatures were, so he was taking no chances. Later he learned that there was nothing to fear from these large birds.

He spent the night near the waterhole, and next day found him wandering more or less aimlessly across the plains, instinctively searching for his lost band of reds. Once, he really did sight a lone red in the distance, but when he hopped towards it, the animal most unsociably took to its legs and vanished southwards.

During the weeks that followed, Joey covered many miles in an unsystematic search, but not one kangaroo did he find. The reason was that, during the time he had been in captivity, regular drives by white settlers had devastated that particular stretch of country, and the larger bands had migrated further west and north.

Though Joey spent a great deal of his time on the plains, he did not altogether neglect the hills. Up to then, however, he had not penetrated very deeply into the ranges. Vaguely, he had come to associate unpleasant things with those hills, but could not remember just what those things were. Men, he knew, were mixed up in it, and also dogs of some kind. Joey's brain was that of an average kangaroo, and he did not dwell on these matters.

During one excursion into the foothills he tried to make friends with a wallaby, but that animal treated him with contempt. It would not even allow him to get near it.

It was now mid-spring, and, deep down in his being, Joey felt a curious stirring. More and more as each day passed, he felt the need of companionship of his own kind, but he could not find it.

Joey's favourite spot in these parts was a small glen which ran rather deeply into the hills, was well grassed and watered and contained a cave several yards deep into one side of the bank. As he fed along the grassy slopes he was aware of intense activity around him. In a nearby bush two wrens were busily engaged in nest building. A pair of kookaburras had already set up home in an excavated white ant's nest high up the side of a tall gum tree, while a golden and blue kingfisher, which he had often noticed along the creek, had a mate with him on his fishing excursions.

Insects hummed in the air round him; little birds sang gaily in the trees and bushes; in fact, the whole world seemed to be vitally alive and happy. In the midst of it all was Joey, a lonely kangaroo, mateless, friendless and deserted. He did not understand it as we humans do, but his instinct told him that things were not as they should be with him. Though he did not want to go, something urged him to leave that beautiful spot and head for the hills.

All that summer Joey ranged the mountains, and, when winter came, he was far to the north. Several times he had sniffed the man-scent, and on the first occasion it had not worried him. But when a flying bullet chipped the bark from a tree under which he was cropping grass, he fled for safety. This happened on the fourth occasion he had sniffed the man-scent and ignored it.

Winter found him in the bush on the opposite side of the ranges, and here he remained for several weeks. Once he was chased by a white man's dog, but he had no trouble in eluding it. The man who accompanied the dog sent a shot after him, and it chipped a piece out of his huge tail—but this did not inconvenience him.

One day he was almost trapped in a little gully by a small party of wandering blacks, but he escaped by hopping over the rocks.

His first big adventure since his capture by the white settler came one day in the waning winter. He had found a stretch of open country and was quietly grazing, when all of a sudden he was startled by the appearance of two white men and three dogs. As soon as the men saw him, they loosed their dogs, and, with these at his heels, and followed by the yelling men, he went flying for his life.

Coming to a stream he attempted to clear it in one huge bound, but miscalculated and landed into the middle of the water. The leading dog, without hesitation, plunged into the stream and attacked him.

Joey received the brute fair on his chest. Automatically he grabbed the dog and hugged it tightly to him with his short front paws. Then, holding it from him and without giving the dog a chance, Joey raised his hind legs, supporting his body on his strong tail, and slashed the dog from throat to tail. The mortally wounded dog fell back into the water, which immediately began to redden. The second dog, more wary, crept cautiously forward, and at the same time one of the men on the bank raised his rifle and fired at Joey.

The kangaroo, his attention diverted by the stinging pain in the lower portion of his body, was unprepared for the attack by the second dog, which sank its teeth into his leg.

Outraged and maddened by the bullet wound, Joey swung round, and, with a mighty bound, reached the bank, the dog still clinging to him. Frantic with pain and rage, he flopped on the ground, the dog under him. The dog yelped and let go, and then Joey deliberately flopped his huge tail down hard on the other animal, winding him.

The men by this time had reached the water, and as Joey raised his hind legs to deal out swift death to the writhing canine on the ground, one of the men fired another shot.

The bullet struck the kangaroo on the right ear, neatly clipping a piece from it. It was enough for Joey. In a few seconds he was flying through the scrub with long bounds, and he did not pause until he reached the shelter of a deep and rocky gorge.

Wounded in two places, Joey felt sick when at length he panted to a halt. Blood dropped down into his eyes from the wounded ear, and the bullet in his leg irked him very much. Alternately he licked his wounds and spent the rest of that day resting.

Joey did not move far from that rocky gorge during the following days, because it was painful for him to do so. His wounded leg had gone stiff, and he could make only little hops as he went along. Happily for him, the wound would not be a permanent handicap, but at present it filled his whole world to the exclusion of most everything else. If he had disliked men and dogs hitherto, he now hated and detested them all.

It was nearly a month before Joey felt anything

like himself again. His ear had healed and the dog-bite troubled him no more. But, more to the point, he could move his wounded leg much more freely.

Bit by bit he made his way deeper into the ranges until he found a good piece of grazing ground, and there he remained. He was lucky enough to discover a large piece of flat, grassy land with a pool of water not so far away, and here he determined to stay for a long time.

CHAPTER VI.

HIS DOMAIN

JOEY was finding life in the hills very hard now. Nature had intended him to inhabit the open forest and not-so-dense foothills, not the rocks and thickets which were the haunts of his black-faced cousins, or the wide, open plains which were the heritage of his red relations. For Joey was a great grey. During her lifetime, his mother had spent her time, not so much on the open plains as in the woody country on the opposite side of the range. She never stayed in the hills, but crossed them as quickly as possible, for a great grey kangaroo cannot move about freely in the rock and valley country.

Joey had crossed the mountains all right on his first trip because he had been fortunate enough to discover less difficult country. When he encountered rough going, he moved slowly along in that manner peculiar to kangaroos, swinging his legs forward between an arch formed by his front paws and tail. Most of the day he spent lying around and lazing his time away, moving off to the flat grassland at sundown.

A favourite haunt was that same grassland where he had dragged himself in his wounded state. Water was not far off, the place was secluded, and in one corner he had established quite an elaborate dust bath. This consisted of a large, circular hole in the ground in which he lazed away the warm days.

A longing for the open forest drew him away from the hills at last. Here he could stretch his legs and indulge in those long bounds which were his birthright. He encountered other greys in the bush, but avoided them; in fact, when they began to get numerous he slowly made his way back to his mountain stronghold.

Travelling mostly by night, he worked his way up through the thickets along a wallaby track, which made the going easier. He did not meet any wallabies during this trek, although once a hardy old wallaroo, which he met on a rough hillside, was minded to try conclusions with him and to dispute his passage. Joey, however, was in no mood to be provoked by wallaroos, and accepted the challenge. It was the old wallaroo, however, who gave in and awarded Joey a bloodless victory. In other words, when the wallaroo saw that Joey was ready for a fight, it turned round and scooted away.

Coming to a clearing, Joey interrupted an interesting boxing match. The contestants were two young wallaroos, and when Joey came on the scene they were grappling with and cuffing each other about the head and shoulders with their short front paws, interspersing this with playful kicks. When they saw Joey they adjourned the combat without going through the ceremony of shaking paws, and fled into the thickets.

Joey watched them go with mild contempt, and proceeded to his favourite grassland, arriving there just as dawn broke. He had travelled most of the night and was feeling tired and irritable; and when he found that, in his absence, some other creature had been using his dust bath, he felt much annoyed. Some ill mannered black-faced kangaroo, or an equally ill-behaved wallaroo, presumably, and, before he would even deign to use the dust bath, Joey kicked most of the surface dirt out of it.

Following a luxurious roll, Joey prepared to laze the day away and then he became aware of a menacing shadow that crossed and re-crossed the clearing. Idly he watched it. The shadow began to circle and to grow bigger. He took stock of it mildly, pricking his ears inquiringly, but was far too lazy, far too comfortable to investigate. Some wandering bird, no doubt. More fool it to fly around in the heat when it could be resting in the trees.

The thought of danger to himself did not enter his mind, so it was with a hoarse cough of surprise that he felt a sharp pain in the top of his head. He sprang up and stood erect in the dusty hole, while the bird which had attacked him—a large wedge-tailed eagle

—whirled high into the sky in preparation for another attack.

Joey raised his head as high as he could to keep track of this new and strange menace, but it was not until the huge bird had dropped screaming on to his shoulders and had sunk its sharp talons into his hide that he knew it was upon him. He tried to shake the bird off, but it viciously pecked his ear. In desperation he hurled himself to the ground, but the bird refused to be dislodged.

In pain and in anger, Joey leaped to his feet and made a dash for the trees and, more by luck than good management, succeeded in smashing his feathered attacker hard against a tree trunk. The eagle screamingly released its hold and whirled off into the blue sky, while Joey cowered down under the trees and scrub and stayed there for two hours.

When at last he deemed it safe to venture forth again there was no sign of the eagle, and, after a cautious survey of the surroundings, he returned to his dust hole. But he was not easy at all, and finally left it for the shelter of the trees. It was evening before he returned again, still feeling a trifle sore, and, when he discovered a large and powerful wallaroo calmly lying in his dust bath, he was indignant. Joey crossed the glade with three long bounds and immediately attacked the wallaroo without challenge. The wallaroo had sprung to its feet as soon as it sighted the kangaroo, and it, too, was filled with indignation.

What right had a grey, a forest dweller, in its domain? Burning with resentment, the wallaroo stood ready to repel this intruder.

Joey made a lightning-fast slash which missed, and then grunted as the wallaroo bit him. He was not used to such tactics and they angered him. He glared at his antagonist, which glared back at him, and then hit him again. Joey did not know that all wallaroos use their teeth a great deal when fighting.

He gave ground slightly, and the wallaroo bounded at him. Joey tensed himself, and, before the unlucky wallaroo knew what was going on, the kangaroo flashed up his hind legs and those murderous nails of his had ripped a long tear in his opponent's stomach.

Coughing and grunting hoarsely, the wallaroo swung round, abandoned the fight, and made for the rocks, where it was impossible for Joey to seek him out. Joey did not attempt to do so. He dismissed the matter from his mind and began to feed. He was not troubled by that wallaroo again.

The mountain creatures did not attempt to fraternise with Joey, nor did he offer them any encouragement to do so. He had no right on those ranges at all, but he was determined to stay there and, if necessary, fight all comers for the privilege. Man rarely penetrated these parts, and this naturally suited Joey.

Periodically, the kangaroo's instinct urged him to

visit the plains and the bush, but he never stayed in either locality for very long. Wise now in the ways of the wild creatures, he knew that the red kangaroos of the open plains would never trouble him. He had only contempt for rock wallabies and wallaroos, and he avoided his own kith and kin, the greys. He rarely left the wooded portions of the opposite slope when he dropped down on the plains side of the range.

No, the mountains would do him. If other creatures resented his presence, let them oust him if they could. He was a grey, a great grey, the king species of all the kangaroos, and if he chose to invade the open plains which belonged to the red kangaroos, the dense thickets where the black kangaroos lived, or the rough hillsides that were the rightful homes of the wallaroos, he would do so. Again, if he wanted to spend portion of his life in the open forest where dwelt his own species, why, who was there to prevent him?

At present he was enjoying the mountains, and though he could not move about as freely as he would like, it was his domain.

CHAPTER VII.

THE KILLER OF DOGS

Whistling cheerfully, the young man made his way to the creek, filled the billy can, and, returning to the camp fire, hung the can on to a piece of S-shaped wire which was depending from a raised triangle of poles. Then he threw a bundle of sticks on the blaze and sat down.

"Do you think there is much chance of us running into him round these parts?" he asked of the party generally, as he filled an old, blackened pipe.

There were four or five men in the party, and one of them grunted.

"I shouldn't think so," he commented as he jabbed a stick into the fire and conveyed it carefully to his pipe. "Bill Pike tells me he was last sighted a month ago in the hills far to the north of here. The chances are that by now he'll be well out on the plains until the winter sets in properly."

"I can't say I can swallow all these yarns I hear about that blessed kangaroo," said one of the men. "I know that a cornered 'roo is sudden death on a dog, but I can't believe that any kangaroo would go out deliberately looking for dogs to kill.

"Hardly that, Tom," smiled a grizzled old man on the other side of the fire; "The yarn is that no dog that has ever pitted himself against this kangaroo has lived. He's sudden death, by all accounts. He has taken on dogs of almost every breed, but the result is the same. I know plenty about 'roos, but I've never yet come across one that lived for nothing but dog killing. You could believe it about some wild animals, but not a kangaroo."

"Bill Pike told me the yarn," put in another of the party. "He was out prospecting with a mate and they had a black retriever with them. Pikey says they ran into this kangaroo and it immediately set upon the dog and killed it."

"I don't swallow that yarn," grinned the old man. "That is most unlike a kangaroo. They don't fight like that."

"Ever seen two kangaroos having a set-to?" asked the young man who had filled the billy can.

"I haven't even seen one tackle a dog."

The grizzled old bushman smiled again.

"I've seen a few," he remarked reminiscently. "They fight in different ways. In the case of a dog, a 'roo will strike it with its heavy tail, but mostly depends on that terrible nail which terminates the fourth toe of the hind leg. The 'roo stands against a tree or against anything handy, leans back on this and supports itself with its tail. It always moves its hind legs together. It can't lean on one and use the other in its fighting.

"In the open country or any place where there are no trees or rocks," he went on, "the 'roo will stand up in the open and use its tail for support. When there is a brawl on between two kangaroos, they stand face to face and tear each other to bits—if they can."

There was silence around the fire. Overhead the stars were beginning to twinkle in a clear sky. At intervals a mopoke croaked mournfully as it winged its way on some nocturnal errand, and the weird cry of a curlew sounded at a distance. The party of men round the fire presented a homely scene. The camp was in a small clearing, and three or four lean-looking greyhound dogs were chained to convenient trees. Now and then there came the musical clinking of hobbled horses.

The men were there for a twofold purpose —primarily they were prospecting, but they intended, if possible, to prove or disprove a mysterious rumour that had been circulating the settled places of the south.

Stories had come through, brought mainly by wandering bushmen and prospectors, of a lone kangaroo that haunted the northern ranges. He was a remarkable marsupial by all accounts, and was sudden death to dogs. Men he detested, and at first sight of them he was up and away. If they had dogs, it was said that he deliberately lured these away and, getting them into some secluded spot, ruthlessly killed them. Fully a dozen men who had visited the hills had stories to tell of an elusive grey kangaroo, close to which it was impossible to get, and of favourite dogs slaughtered by it.

Old bushmen and settlers who knew kangaroos treated the stories with contempt, but rumour persisted, and now a party of prospectors were determined to devote part of their trip to searching out this mysterious grey phantom.

The trouble was to locate him. He had been seen, according to rumour, in the hills to the north, the bush to the east, and the plains to the west—a huge grey kangaroo in the very prime of life, one ear half missing, and what appeared to be a scarred leg. Nobody had got close enough to investigate that scar, but those who had managed to see him at all were unanimous about the chipped-off ear.

Early next morning the party was astir. Horses were saddled, camping gear packed, dogs loosed, and a start made for the first foothills. After travelling for two days the party established a permanent camp in a glade where the bush joined the lower foothills. That part of the country had never been frequented by man, except a few wandering blacks, until a few years previously, when rumours of gold had attracted a few prospectors.

Most of the winter was spent by the party among the hills. They met with indifferent success from a gold-winning point of view. Of the mysterious kangaroo they saw nothing. In the early spring they moved north about ten miles, and established a new camp. By this time all thoughts of the kangaroo had been driven from their heads by the discovery of payable gold in the mountain streams.

One evening the leader of the party, the old bushman, Ben Onslow, was returning to camp after a day in the upper reaches of the creek, when he noticed a footprint in the mud. A close scrutiny revealed it as the pad mark of a large kangaroo. He reported the incident to the camp when he arrived, and it was discussed with some interest around the fire that night.

Next morning, when the young billy-boiler was feeding the dogs he found that one was missing. It was a lean brindle kangaroo dog, the property of old Onslow. He thought nothing of the matter, as the dog was no doubt handy in the bush, and contented himself with cursing the missing animal.

A start on the day's work was made shortly after breakfast, and all hands had strict instructions to keep a lookout for kangaroo sign—and also the missing dog. Old Onslow muttered dark things about the dog as he headed into the hills, shovel over his shoulder.

Reaching the scene of the day's work, he was soon

busily panning the silt from the bottom of the stream. His location was a natural grotto. The creek tumbled noisily over a small precipice and ran down the gully to where the rest of the prospectors were working.

After he had panned a few shovelfuls, he straightened up and lit his pipe. His eyes wandered absently to the top of the gully on the left side, and what he saw made him catch his breath.

Calmly watching him, actually gazing down at him with an inquiring expression on its face, was a huge grey kangaroo with half of one ear missing.

"Well, what do you know about that?" he stuttered to himself.

The kangaroo eyed him for a moment and then, as Onslow made a sudden movement, it vanished.

Hastily he rushed to the bank and scrambled up it. He caught sight of a grey form vanishing round a rock and he gave chase. Of course, it was hopeless, and as he came to a halt with a grin, he wondered what had made him chase the thing. Dropping to a walk, he kept on going for a few minutes, but the kangaroo had gone.

Smiling to himself, but excited nevertheless, Onslow turned and ran along the top of the gully towards where his comrades were working, intent on telling them what he had seen.

Rounding a rock which towered twenty feet above

his head, he got a rude shock. There, lying on the ground in front of him, a pitiful heap, was his favourite dog, Peter, the missing greyhound. It was easy to see how he had died. The long rip in the breast told its own story. Peter, evidently, had gone out hunting early, had encountered the fiendish killer, chased it to the rock, where it had turned at bay.

The old man, cursing himself for not having tied the dog up before he sought his bunk the previous night, knelt at its side. It was quite dead. Quietly he picked up the animal and carried it silently down the gully to where his friends were working.

"Boys," he said grimly, "no more prospecting for me until that kangaroo is dead. Poor old Peter! And to think that, after it had killed my pal, that kangaroo came and sneered at me as I worked!"

His friends attempted to console him, but he would have none of their sympathy. The dog was buried on the bank of the creek. Old Onslow did not work any more that day. He spent it in camp cleaning his double-barrelled shot gun and his repeating rifle, and vowing dire vengeance on the killer of his greyhound dog.

CHAPTER VIII.

THE HUNT

JOEY was a far different kangaroo now from the terrified creature that had lain panting at the end of two ropes when caught by the white man years before. He was no longer the lonely marsupial searching for his lost species. Lonely he was in fact, but his yearning for company was completely eradicated.

It was now several years since he had lost portion of his ear and received the bullet wound in his leg. When he had dragged himself to the patch of grassland on the top of the range that day, he had been a sick and sorry animal. At first his wound troubled him, but as time wore on, it grew less troublesome, and at length inconvenienced him not at all.

As one year gave way to another, Joey grew and grew, and his solitude grew with him. Periodically he made pilgrimages to the bush and occasionally came across others of his kind, but he did not associate with them. True, at times he did linger with a mob, but was never part of it. Haughty and aloof was Joey, unsociable and alone. He had no aspirations to mate with any of them, or to lead any mob. Once his presence was resented by an old kangaroo who was the acknowledged leader, and in the resultant fight, Joey gave him a thorough beating. That meant that the leadership was his if he wanted it, but Joey would have none of the homage the mob was prepared to accord him. His earlier experiences seemed to cut him off from the rest of the kangaroo world, and as he grew older, a strange content settled upon him.

No longer did he fear man as he had feared him in the days that were past and gone. He distrusted man, and always made himself scarce when humans were about. As for dogs, they were beneath his notice. He had had several contests with them and had found victory easy.

Joey remembered the black retriever belonging to the man, Bill Pike. It had followed him until it had got him into a corner from which he could not escape, so he had turned round and killed it. There had been nothing else to do. It had been his life or the dog's. The retriever had been no fighter at all. Other dogs he had met had been poor fighters, too. He recalled bouts with sheepdogs and kelpies—easy kills. Dingoes were troublesome, and unless he met one alone he did not give battle. Greyhounds troubled him. He had had one rather tough battle with a greyhound in the shallow waters of a creek, and he did not desire a repetition of that.

Men were more numerous in the hills now, and
Joey began to spend a great deal of his days in the
bush. Each winter, however, found him in his familiar
mountains—in fact, he was a creature of habit. Spring
he passed in the bush, summer and autumn on the
fringe of the plains and the foothills, and winter, in
the deepest part of the ranges.

And so his life went on.

Joey had received a great surprise that day when he
had gone to the little waterfall for a drink and had
found old Onslow in occupation. It was coming on
spring, and Joey had been making down out of the
hills to the bush. As he hopped away after seeing
Onslow, he remembered the exciting fight he had had
that very morning.

When the first grey streaks of dawn had lightened
the eastern sky, he had headed for the gully in search
of water. He had been in the higher hills for the past
few weeks, and consequently had not known that the
creek for which he had been heading had been taken
over by gold-seeking white men.

He had not seen the greyhound dog until he was
on top of it as the wind was blowing in the wrong
direction. On the other hand, Peter, the greyhound,
had discovered him and was seeking him out.

Joey rounded the giant rock much in the same
manner as old Onslow did some hours later, with this
difference—Joey had hopped while the old man

walked. He received the dog full in the breast before he even knew it was there. The dog sprang at him like a brindle avalanche. Experienced, and now proof against surprise, Joey clouted the dog on the side of the head with a powerful front paw. The dog fell back, but immediately came again, this time sinking its teeth into Joey's big tail. With a mighty heave he threw the dog off and prepared for its next attack.

The dog was not slow to reply. It threw itself at Joey again and was knocked backwards by a flashing front paw. Before it could recover, the kangaroo, now thoroughly angered, gave a short bound and was on the greyhound. It swerved away and then came at Joey in crawling fashion, its belly on the ground. Obviously it intended to creep under the kangaroo's paws and then thrust itself upwards in an effort to reach Joey's throat. Nothing suited Joey better. He embraced the dog tightly and lifted those terrible hind legs armed with razor-sharp, death-dealing claws. fiercely the dog struggled, and Joey lost his grip just long enough for the lithe greyhound to wriggle free.

As the dog fell to the ground, Joey pushed the war into its territory. He made a bound at the dog, which swerved sideways in the very nick of time. Joey missed with his claws, but his big tail thumped down on the dog with a sickening thud. The dog yelped and crawled out of range, two ribs broken.

Again the kangaroo leaped, but the dog was quicker, in spite of its hurts, and, with a mighty effort, gathered its remaining strength for a final spring. Joey received it and grasped it in a bear-like hug. The dog was now past active resistance, and it was all over in a few seconds.

Joey gazed at his dead enemy for a few seconds in unconscious tribute to a very brave and worthy foe, and then wandered off towards the little waterfall. It was then that he saw old Onslow and old Onslow saw him.

After this sudden surprise of seeing the old white man, he hopped away along a spur which led downwards, and in due course reached the fringe of the bush. Into the forest he plunged and was soon making a leisurely journey through the trees, unconsciously setting a course in a north-easterly direction towards the far-distant creek, where he had spent his early days. He was not going there, however. Joey hardly ever had any set plans, except his seasonal migrations.

The course he set, though it lay in the direction of his early home, also took him towards the camp of the prospectors. He sensed it long before he came to it, and after a cursory glance, skirted it and continued his north-easterly trek. By the time old Onslow and his party were ready to search the hills, Joey was miles away in the opposite direction.

Back in the camp, the old man had persuaded the rest of the party to cease work for the day to go with him kangaroo-hunting. It was noon before they got a start on, and they commenced their search at the top of the gully where Joey had lingered to study old Onslow. The dogs were eager for the trail, and within a few minutes the whole party, fully armed and with the dogs at leash in case of a sudden encounter with the hunted kangaroo, were on the trail.

For some time all went well, and then the scent was lost on the rocky ground. A great deal of time was wasted in picking it up again.

It was late in the afternoon when they found themselves back in the bush, and learned with great surprise and indignation that the kangaroo had actually been at their camp, or at least within a few hundred yards of it, without the dogs knowing. It was useless proceeding any further that day, so the party entered their camp, resolved to spend the whole of the following day on the trail.

During the night, Joey ranged the bush within a few miles' radius of the camp, always keeping well to windward. The feed was excellent, and his small brain did not convey to the rest of him enough intelligence to make him get out of the way while the going was good. He was a hardy and experienced animal, but in many ways he was a fool.

It was not surprising, therefore, that the party of

white men found little difficulty next morning in locating fresh tracks, but with the coming of the new day, Joey had moved off in a more or less straight course, north-westerly. All that morning he kept on, with the party behind him, but this time he did not have the wind in his favour. He was quite unaware of the pursuit.

While he preserved a dawdling pace, the pursuers moved fast, and by noon they were within shouting distance of him. A break in the bush for several miles gave him away.

As he was crossing this wide, open space, he was sighted by the men behind. He was travelling slowly, picking at the grass as he went, and the wind did not help him. A rapid calculation told the men that if the kangaroo kept up his present pace, it would take him half-an-hour to cross the wide glade and reach the bush beyond. The opportunity for them was a golden one, and they did not want to spoil it by precipitate action. Old Onslow, who had the death of his dog to spur him on, advised that the whole of the dogs be unleashed and sent in full cry after Joey, but their various owners, crouching on the ground by their hounds and holding their muzzles to prevent an alarm being raised, dissented vigorously. They did not want their animals killed.

One of the party was in favour of stalking the kangaroo until a favourable opportunity of shooting him presented itself.

"Why on earth didn't we bring the horses?" moaned old Onslow. "We could have run him down easily."

"Let the dogs loose. Four of them ought to keep him occupied until we can get within range with our rifles," said one of the men who did not own a dog.

This started an argument between the men who did, and while the party discussed the pros and cons, Joey progressed steadily towards the bush. The men could see that something would have to be done at once.

Then old Onslow put forward a plan. It was that two of the men with their dogs should make a wide detour and try to get in front of the kangaroo, with the object of turning him back. In this manner he would be trapped between two fires. The plan was rapidly approved of, and as rapidly put into action, two of the men vanishing into the bush on one side.

Joey, in no hurry, idly fed on. The watching men behind waited with bated breath. The two men who were making the detour were experienced bushmen who could be depended upon not to make a hash of the plan. Joey unwittingly assisted the scheme by remaining in one spot for fully five minutes.

With their eyes glued upon him, the waiting men behind saw the kangaroo suddenly raise his head and stare fixedly in front of him. At almost the same moment two long, lithe hounds shot out of the bush and made for him like arrows from two bows.

"Let go your dogs! Let them loose!" screamed old Onslow in an agony of excitement to the two men with him. They did so swiftly.

With two greyhounds rushing him from either side, and with shouting white men, seemingly all around him, Joey was in the greatest predicament of his adventurous life. He swung round to face the peril from the right, and then became urgently aware of the one on his left. The dogs which had made the detour were the nearest to him, and upon these he turned.

Reared up to his full height, and with the light of battle flaring in his eyes, he met the attack of the first dog by swerving sharply. The animal shot past him. The second one he cleared with a hop, and then made straight for the on-coming men.

Wildly one of them fired, but the bullet sped harmlessly by. The other pulled trigger when Joey was only twenty yards away, and, by a strange coincidence, drilled a hole through what remained of the kangaroo's mutilated ear.

With a bound, Joey was upon them. Both men dropped to their knees to take fresh aim, and then, gathering himself together, the kangaroo, with one mighty and magnificent leap, cleared both their heads with feet to spare, and was gone into the bush beyond.

"Good heavens!" exclaimed one of the men, awestruck, as he got to his feet and wiped his brow with the back of his hand. "Did you see it?"

His comrade nodded vigorously.

"It passed over my head like a great grey cloud. I thought it was going to attack us," he said.

By this time the rest of the party had reached them and the dogs were all securely tied to prevent any pursuit, which might end in disaster for them. In a group the men stood and discussed the amazing thing they had witnessed. They were satisfied now, they confessed to each other, that all the stories they had heard about that kangaroo were true.

"Do you know," one of them said at last, "it seems a pity to hunt that animal after this."

Old Onslow nodded his grizzled head.

"Yes," he said slowly, "the thing got my dog, Peter, but I'm not going to hold it against him any more. No doubt poor Peter got what he was looking for. I, for one, am not going to hunt that 'roo any more."

For the rest of their stay in that part of the country, the prospectors did not trouble to look for Joey. In any case, had they done so, they would have searched in vain, because that kangaroo was no longer there.

For spring was waning, and Joey was due for the plains.

CHAPTER IX.

KING OF THE RANGES

AHEAD of Joey was a long and tedious journey over the ranges before he could reach the plains, but that did not worry him. His time was his own. On those plains he could really stretch himself. He was a self-sufficient animal, not given to profound thoughts. Scientists would have told him that he was a Macropus Giganteus of the order Marsupiata, but that would not have interested him. Scientists would have also told him that he was a giant grey kangaroo which, when put to it, could traverse space with the rapidity of an arrow, clearing as much as thirty feet in length in a single bound and jumping from six to ten feet in height. Joey knew all that without being told, but he did not know he was a fool.

For he was a fool. No grey kangaroo with any sense would have chosen the life he had, living in mountains in preference to the bush and avoiding his own kind. And, in addition to being a fool, Joey was rapidly becoming an old man—a rather nasty old man at that.

Up on the ranges, his favourite spot was the grassland to which he had dragged himself that day long ago when he had received the bullet wound, and thither he made his leisurely way.

In due course he arrived and, when he did, he found distinct kangaroo signs. This annoyed him intensely. These mountains were his own special domain and intruders were unwelcome. The fact that he himself might not be welcome on the plains or in the bush, or even in these very ranges, had absolutely nothing to do with it. Let them all keep out of these hills.

There were undoubted signs that another grey kangaroo, probably with friends, which made the crime worse, had been visiting his mountain retreat. This was something not to be tolerated. Had he ever foisted himself upon any other kangaroos? No, he had not, and he would not have any strangers using his particular stretch of grassland in these ranges.

Joey browsed around the spot for some days, but no other marsupial put in an appearance. Gradually his resentment subsided, and he began to contemplate continuing his journey down to the plains. But before he went, he felt he would like to make certain that the unwelcome visitor or visitors had left his grassland for good. If they were still there, well, they would have to be ousted, and taught such a lesson that they would think twice -about returning. He would not deliberately go looking for fight, he told himself. That was not his way; but if any other animal aspired to mortal combat, so much the worse for him.

Such was Joey's state of mind these days. Ever since he had left his mother's side, all too soon, he had had to fight his way through a bitter world, and it was Fate that had made him an outcast.

At the end of a week he decided to travel down to the plains. Taking his time over the trip, he gradually dropped down and down until he reached a valley which led out on to level ground. He was almost out of it before he scented danger. He did not quite know what it was, but he sensed it, and became cautious.

A vagrant wind played him false, and the first hint of real danger was conveyed to him by ear—the barking of a dog. Dogs meant men! He stiffened in his tracks, standing rigid like a great grey ghost in the gathering dusk.

Bang! There was no mistaking that noise! He did not stop to make inquiries, but swung around and was off up the gully like a streak. So there were white men on the plains! Was there any place on earth where these white men and their dogs and guns did not go? There was nothing for it but to seek the safety of the ranges once more.

The next few days he spent aimlessly wandering the bushy mountain creeks and gullies, and then the urge drove him to his favourite grassland.

Before he reached it he knew it was occupied, and,

when he broke through the trees, he was not surprised to find a large old kangaroo grazing there. The intruder viewed his arrival with distrust.

Joey bounded lightly to the centre of the glade, and, dropping down on his front paws, began to nibble the grass, using a funny little kind of walk as he moved about. The other kangaroo did likewise, and they both moved round the glade in a circle, the stranger in front a few yards.

Joey increased his pace slightly, and so did the other. Then he changed his tactics. He gradually turned around and began a fresh circuit in the opposite direction, a course which, if the other did not change direction, would eventually bring them face to face.

But the other old man was alive to the manoeuvre, and swung round, too. For ten minutes they kept up this grim game of follow-my-leader, and then Joey got tired of it.

Suddenly he raised himself to his full height and thumped his great tail on the ground several times. It was a gesture of direct defiance to the unwelcome visitor, who was not slow in acknowledging it.

It was a grand sight to see those two hardy old bush creatures each raised to its full stature, glaring defiance at each other. There they stood, separated by not more than twenty feet, watching each other's slightest movement—ever on the alert. Joey, his front paws idly dangling in apparent unreadiness, saw a sudden stiffening of the muscles of his opponent's hind legs. The moment for battle had come!

Joey did not wait for the coming attack, but launched himself through the air, taking the initiative. At almost the exact second, his antagonist took off. They met in mid-air with a thunderous impact, which threw them both backwards. Recovering swiftly, they stood and faced each other with twitching ears, and front paws working convulsively. Joey gave two small hops which brought him to within a few feet of the other. Leaning back to give his great tail the full support of his body, he raised both hind feet off the ground and slashed. His wary old opponent, expecting the move, threw himself backwards, pivoted in the same movement, and whirled his great tail round in a sweeping arc. Joey leaped back, but did not get quite out of range, the flying tail stinging his flank like the cut of a whiplash.

Infuriated by this reverse, and before the other could regain his poise, he leaped in closer, and got in a deft slash. This maddened the recipient, who returned furiously to the battle, and then they stood up to each other and slashed away, each intent upon ripping the other to pieces.

Suddenly they gave way and fell back, sides heaving. It was honours even. The breathing space was brief, both flying in to attack again as if actuated by the one spring. This time Joey succeeded in shrewdly ripping the other, a wound which shook him badly. He replied with a vicious double slash, and then they fell to work with a vengeance.

But the end was not far off. His antagonist was weakening, and Joey himself was in no shape to prolong the struggle. Calling up all his strength for one supreme effort, Joey succeeded in his aim to doubly rip his opponent's belly. The invader of his sacred domain slipped sideways and fell to the grass.

The victorious Joey did not know the meaning of the term "chivalry." He deliberately turned round and, with the last atoms of strength he possessed, brought his big tail down with a series of whacks on his dying opponent, crushing the last vestige of life from him. Then, with a mighty sigh, he himself dropped to the ground, overcome by his wounds.

Hour succeeded hour, but still he lay there side by side with his vanquished foe, getting weaker and weaker. At last he managed to drag himself swaying to his feet, and, half-lurching, half-hopping, staggered away from the scene of battle. Through the bushes and rocks he went, leaving a trail of blood behind, and, reaching a small water-hole, drank and drank. On again, slowly and painfully, until he reached his objective—a small cave in an almost inaccessible part of the range—and there he dropped.

It was many days before he was anything like himself again. A merciful nature preserved him, but, unless miracles were performed upon those age-old mountains, he would never again be the wonderful fighting machine he had been.

When he felt fit to range again, winter was upon him, adding to his troubles. And what a sight he was these days! One ear gone, chest and belly scarred and torn, a deep wound scarcely healed in one leg, an old bullet wound in the other thigh, gaunt, grey, and feeling indescribably old.

Throughout that winter, which, mercifully, was very mild, and well into the succeeding spring, Joey kept to the hills, nursing his wounds and regaining his lost strength. Bodily ills prevented him from travelling as had been his custom—to the plains and the bush after the choicest grasses and food, and he was forced to exist on the scanty food that the ranges provided.

True, there was not one living creature in those ranges, wandering humans excepted, that dared to face him, for Joey had a reputation, a well-earned reputation; yet, what a price he had paid for it!

King of the Ranges!

But...

He did not re-visit the scene of that last battle. Instead, he wandered to the northward, keeping always to the hills, and then he was fortunate enough to find another grassy patch, which suited him very well. Here he remained for several weeks.

One beautiful evening as he went down to the water to drink, he saw by the signs around the hole that another kangaroo had been there. Joey was in a dilemma. He was as yet in no shape for fighting, even though his last battle had been fought months before. He stayed only long enough to satisfy his thirst, and then, without returning to his patch of grassland, struck eastwards, heading for the bush. Here he remained for a month until he met other kangaroos, and this forced him back into his beloved hills. But here again were kangaroo signs. So Joey moved on again.

He was still deliberately avoiding his kind, as he had done since his early days, but now he had a different reason. Hitherto it had been from choice. Now it was because of necessity. For the first time since he had grown to full adult size and age, Joey feared a meeting with another kangaroo. For the first time, too, he had no great faith in himself.

If he had any kingship over these ranges, it was swiftly coming to an end.

CHAPTER X.

WANING DAYS

AS the sun sank behind the distant hills, the black kangaroo left the patch of thick scrub in which he had been lying during the day. He made slowly across an open space towards the neighbouring stream where the long river grass attracted him, then became aware of a movement in the thickets to the left of him.

He pricked up his ears, and, after gazing fixedly at the spot for several seconds, gave the ground two inquiring thumps with his tail. His inquiry was answered by a similar duet, so he sat back on his haunches and waited.

Out of the thickets, in a deferential kind of way, hopped an old grey kangaroo, one ear missing, the front portion of his body badly scarred.

The black kangaroo stiffened slightly and made a tentative half-turn as if contemplating flight, but the old stranger dropped down on his forepaws and began to nibble the grass.

The black kangaroo could not get the drift of it at all. Here was a great, grey old man, a redoubtable warrior from all appearances, and, therefore, one to be treated with the greatest respect, acting like a half-

scared joey. What was the game? The black kangaroo
distrusted Joey and, with a flick of its tail, bolted into
the scrub.

Joey was relieved. As he approached the spot he
had been aware of the other's presence. The place was
attractive and was big enough for the two of them.
He did not want to fight for it, so had adopted a
conciliatory, attitude.

He need not have gone to all that trouble. The
black kangaroo had had no use for that open place.
He had merely been crossing it to reach a much more
desirable feeding ground. He did not care who used
it. Joey did not know all this, of course, and was
inclined to preen himself.

He browsed slowly around until dark and then set
off for the waterhole. In this open forest he could
move quickly, and off he went in the direction the
black kangaroo had taken earlier.

Less than ten minutes' travelling brought him to
the banks of a fairly wide creek, and he drank his fill
without interruption. As he turned away to return to
the forest he became aware of a small mob of
kangaroos, making for the stream further along.
They, too, saw him, but did not heed him.

Some latent instinct compelled him to move
towards them, but he did not proceed in direct hops.
He dropped on his front paws and fed his way along
in the fashion peculiar to his kind, and when within a

hundred yards of them he stopped and fed in the one spot.

There were eight in the mob, and they were greys —his own people. The leader was a large young 'roo, and he did not like Joey.

Joey did not mingle with the mob as they fed along the stream. When they approached him, he moved away a bit, intending to convey that he did not want to interfere with them.

The leader took stock of him narrowly, and saw before him a mighty old warrior who, obviously, had seen better days, but who might be a very ugly customer in a free-for-all fight. This inventory made him feel uneasy. He did not want to have to fight Joey, in whom he saw a likely rival for the mob leadership, yet he did not want to lose that leadership. He had only held it three days. The previous leader was skulking somewhere in the bush, having been soundly trounced by the young upstart now worrying his head over Joey.

He would have been greatly relieved had he known what Joey's attitude was. Joey wanted nothing but peace and quiet. Several times in his life he had proved that, though he was a most efficient fighter, he had no brains. In him the instinct of self-preservation was not singularly developed. He did not have enough sense to keep out of danger unless that danger was literally thrust under his nose.

When he left the hills it was because he could no

longer defend his kingship. He had had enough instinct to leave a place where he had been unfitted by nature to live when his own natural gifts had failed him. In coming to the open forest, he had done the best thing in the circumstances. An animal with sense would have acknowledged himself beaten after he had gone through as much as Joey. Certainly, no sagacious animal would join up with a mob led by a youngster full of fight. But Joey was a fool of a kangaroo. Instead of keeping to himself, he was deliberately jeopardising his declining years by attempting to make friends with a species from which he voluntarily had alienated himself, and with which he was out of sympathy.

Perhaps it would not be strictly accurate to say that Joey actually wanted to chum up with this band of kangaroos, but in some indefinable way their presence was comforting. He had noticed the fine young leader, and really and honestly believed that, if it came to a stand-up battle, he could beat the youngster. It would, he thought, be age and experience against youth and inexperience, With the odds on the former. But Joey did not desire to fight. He had it all worked out in his 'roo way—if he showed by his actions that he did not wish to molest anyone, or to be molested, he might be permitted to feed about in peace.

He should have known better.

Several of the mob began to straggle back towards

the forest, and the last to leave was the young leader. He was in a dilemma. He did not want to fight Joey, but he was determined to keep an eye on him. Joey followed them slowly for a few hundred yards and then turned aside, hopping down to the lower end of the belt of trees where the grass looked good to him. He left behind him a very relieved mob leader.

He did not leave the stream that night, and next morning found him back at the place where the mob had been feeding on the previous evening. They did not return there that day, and, towards sunset, Joey entered the forest and pushed in a north-easterly direction.

He discovered kangaroo signs in several open spaces, but it was old. In one spot he found several luxurious dustholes and, selecting the largest one, lazed into it. Night came down, and he left the hole for water, but returned again and spent most of the night browsing. Next day he gave over to lazing in the dusthole.

Towards the evening of the fourth day of his having discovered this pleasant spot, he was momentarily startled by the arrival of a mob of six greys, who entered the clearing and regarded him with great distrust. Only one of them was old—a mother with a young joey in her pouch. They accepted Joey's presence without enthusiasm. Some of them relaxed into dustholes, while others fed around.

At sundown, two others arrived, and one of them was the acknowledged leader of the mob. It was the same animal that Joey had met four days earlier.

When he saw Joey reclining in a dusthole that he himself had long before taken over as his own, the mob leader was indignant. It would never do, he told himself, to let the matter pass. What would his mob think of him if he ignored this slight upon his personal honour and dignity?

He bounded across the clearing and, pausing within ten feet of the lazing Joey, who did not trouble to rise, banged his tail twice on the ground—the direct challenge to combat.

Joey slowly raised himself to his full height, and ran a calculating eye over his younger adversary. Joey was feeling pretty fit now, but did not want to fight unless he had to. The other kangaroo did not want to fight either, but he had to. He wanted to remain king of his mob.

The mob leader opened the battle by sparring at Joey in a manner reminiscent of a boxer. Joey did not move. Encouraged, the younger animal emitted a hoarse, coughing sound, and made a slash at him. Joey propped back, and the blow missed.

This was only the second fight in the youngster's career, and Joey's seeming reluctance encouraged him. Joey, however, was now determined to fight if the other forced battle upon him. He would not turn tail.

For, though Joey was a deposed monarch and also

a fool, and preferred nothing so much as peace and quiet these days, and though the old vengeful lust of battle had died down within him, something in his brain kept hammering out the thought: the King of the Ranges must not be worsted by the cocky young leader of a band of eight.

So, when the youngster gave him a sharp pat with a front paw, Joey decided to risk it, and give battle. With something like his old fire and dash, he suddenly propped back on his tail and made a feinting slash. The leader avoided it easily, and replied by tearing open one of Joey's ancient wounds.

That hurt. Joey did not see plain red — he glimpsed a patch of vivid scarlet. In a flash he was on his opponent, rage bringing to him much of his old-time prowess. From then onwards it was merely a massacre, as Joey, possessed of a devil, gave the youngster no quarter. When, at last, he sank to the ground, Joey hopped over the prostrate body and crushed the life out of it with a series of savage blows from his big tail.

Swinging round, he contemplated the rest of the mob as if bent on committing assault and battery on them all. He made a long leap at a small male, which eluded him and fled into the bush on the wings of terror. The others were not slow to follow, and, within a few seconds, Joey had the place to himself, except for his dead companion.

Joey did not deign to throw the fallen one a second glance, but went, with dignified hops, across the ground to the opposite side, to drop into a dusthole recently quitted by a terror-stricken 'roo when Joey had first exhibited signs of running amok. His eye wandered round the clearing with haughty stare, but there was none to dispute him.

CHAPTER XI.

JOEY COMES HOME

HIS newly returned dignity full upon him, Joey left the clearing at dawn and, keeping to the denser portions of the bush, set a course due north. Once he coughed belligerently at an inoffensive goanna sunning itself on a hollow log, and the goanna, feeling abashed, scampered up the nearest tree.

All that day he kept steadily onwards, and night found him well on his journey. Two wandering dingoes chased him for several miles just before dusk. Joey allowed them to do so until he got tired of the game. He killed one in the orthodox manner, while the other was biting at him. He leaped into a shallow creek with the second one still tearing at him and, grabbing it with his paws, forced it under water and held it there until it drowned.

For almost a week he travelled. Speed became essential one day when he was forced out of a patch of bracken by a bush fire which almost caught him as he slept, and on another occasion he had trouble with sandflies when he was foolish enough to linger around a swamp area where the grass was long and easy to get.

And then one day Joey came home.

How many years before was it that he had played along the banks of this little stream by his mother's side, spending carefree hours safe in the knowledge of her protecting presence? For, if Joey had a real home, it was this pretty little winding creek; and, like the wanderer on the face of the earth; he had returned.

But what a return! Many years ago a sprightly young kangaroo, sprightly in the very joy of living, had departed these sunny places for a far destination, snug in a maternal pouch. Years later he had returned, a battered old gaunt and grey kangaroo, one ear missing, body rent and torn by many a battle, leg and tail scarred by white men's bullets, hide bitten by tame dog and warrigal—an ancient warrior returning to the haunts of his childhood days.

And then it rained. For three weeks Joey did not stir far from a little patch of fern and timber which he discovered after a lot of searching among the scrubby woodlands and forests. The little stream was converted into a rushing torrent in the first few days. At the end of the week it was in rapid flood. This drove Joey eventually further into the bush, but at last rain was displaced by sunshine, and he was back at his creek.

Three miles below where he then was, the creek entered a small swamp area, and thither Joey made his way. The hot sun had caused thousands of sandflies to gather, and they hailed Joey's advent with joy. They stung him until they could sting no longer, and he was forced to tear himself away from the luscious grass and retire to the dense bush. When his eyes were better again he moved up the stream some miles above the swamp and arrived at a clearing in which several other kangaroos were feeding. A fierce old male immediately thumped a warning and a challenge, but Joey ignored him, to take stock of the clearing. There were six kangaroos there, including the old male. They were all well grown, four being females and the other two males.

Joey began to graze among them and presently, to his surprise, he felt something soft nuzzling him. He looked up inquiringly. It was a beautiful dove-coloured female kangaroo, and she obviously wanted to be friendly. Joey nuzzled her and she nuzzled him again, and they might have kept this up indefinitely had not Joey's attention been distracted by an annoying sound of persistent drumming. What could it be?

There was little doubt what it was. The old male kangaroo was still issuing challenges to fight.

Joey, gently pushing the female kangaroo aside, hopped over to where the old man was still banging his tail on the ground, and looked at him inquiringly. The old man returned the look. Joey twitched his one remaining ear. The old man twitched his two. They stood taking stock of each other for some minutes, Joey posing haughtily, and the old man, still tail thumping, not quite so belligerent.

The other kangaroos, looking on with interest, knew just what the position amounted to. The old male, their leader, warlike enough when Joey had arrived, was now trying to discover some means of withdrawing from his challenge. On the other hand, Joey, conscious of the tender looks the female kangaroo was giving him, was ready for anything.

For a great change had come over the battered old wanderer. Deposed Range King he might be, nearing the end of his days he might be, too, but the soft eyes and soft nose of a lady 'roo had accomplished in a few minutes what long years of bitter warring with nature had failed to do. Joey was, at last, among his own kind and in his proper sphere. For the first time since he had left his mother's side, he had known kindness, and it had filled him full of new life.

That being the case, he was not going to allow this old animal to deprive him of his good luck.

They stood looking each other over for another minute or two, and then Joey acted. He did not bound at the other old animal, neither did he slash him and tear at him with his terrible hind claws. Instead, he gave a sudden pivot, swung round in a half-circle, and banged the other 'roo with his tail. It was a contemptuous blow, but the old man did not resent it. He gave a surprised grunt as the blow made him stagger, and then he turned round and hopped away disconsolately. They saw him no more.

Standing in the middle of the clearing, Joey was conscious of his amiable and gentle mate at his side. Truly, it had been a case of love at first sight! The other four 'roos gathered round them as if in congratulation, and then broke off to feed individually.

Joey and his new friend kept close together, the old King and his beautiful subject. Joey was content.

Far to the west the sun was setting in a blaze of golden glory. Overhead flew a flock of wild fowl to their nesting places in the high trees. Mournfully a mopoke greeted the coming night, while a sleepy kookaburra gave a last tired chuckle ere he fluffed out his feathers in preparation for slumber.

Momentarily a faint breeze set the leaves in the high trees whispering to each other, and then, with a last spasm of brightness, as if loath to leave the already darkening sky, the sun turned the blood-red clouds into a vivid orange which bathed the clearing in soft bright light, relieved by patches of living grey —a contented band of grazing kangaroos.

In the hearts of these placid animals there was nothing but peace; and in the heart of one of them a great joy.

The King of the Ranges had, at last, found his true kingdom.

THE END.

Also available form Living Book Press -

<u>Richard Halliburton's Book of Marvels - The Occident</u>
Join famous adventurer Richard Halliburton as he takes you on a journey to the wonders found in the Americas and Europe. You'll never see the world the same way after touring with Halliburton.

<u>Richard Halliburton's Book of Marvels - The Orient</u>
The adventure continues through Africa and Asia.

<u>Magic Australia - Nuri Mass</u>
See the magic of Australia with Del and his friend Bushbo as they explore from Broome to the Barrier Reef meeting strange charaters like Opal, Nullarbor, Willie Wille the whirlwind and many more.

<u>The Little Grammar People - Nuri Mass</u>
Learn all about the parts of our language in the Kingdom of Grammar. Meet Master Noun, Miss Verb, Little Boy Interjection and many more.

Plus more great titles from C.K. Thompson like-
<u>Maggie the Magnificent</u> and <u>Old Bob's Birds</u>

WWW.LIVINGBOOKPRESS.COM